Magic Tricks

LEVEL 7

/g/

DECODABLES

BY jump!

Teaching Tips

Turquoise Level 7

This book focuses on the grapheme **/g/**.

Before Reading

- Discuss the title. Ask readers what they think the book will be about. Have them support their answer.
- Ask readers to sort the words on page 3. Read the words together. Reinforce that /g/ can have a hard /g/ sound or a soft /j/ sound.

Read the Book

- Encourage readers to read independently, either aloud or silently to themselves.
- Prompt readers to break down unfamiliar words into units of sound and string the sounds together to form the words. Then, ask them to look for context clues to see if they can figure out what these words mean. Discuss new vocabulary to confirm meaning.
- Urge readers to point out when the focused phonics grapheme appears in the text. Does it have a hard /g/ sound or a soft /j/ sound?

After Reading

- Ask readers comprehension questions about the book. In what ways were people in the book performing magic tricks?
- Encourage readers to think of other words with the /g/ grapheme. On a separate sheet of paper, have them write the words in two columns: one for the hard /g/ sound and the other for the soft /j/ sound.

North American adaptations © 2024 Jump!
5357 Penn Avenue South
Minneapolis, MN 55419
www.jumplibrary.com

Library of Congress Cataloging-in-Publication Data is available at www.loc.gov or upon request from the publisher.

ISBN: 979-8-88524-772-6 (hardcover)
ISBN: 979-8-88524-773-3 (paperback)
ISBN: 979-8-88524-774-0 (ebook)

Photo Credits

Images are courtesy of Shutterstock.com. Cover –Sunny studio, p4–5 –Nagy-Bagoly Arpad, Fer Gregory. p6–7 –Robert Kneschke, NSingh Photography. p8–9 –Mark Williams Pics, Dmytro Surkov. p10–11 –Pixel-Shot, Fer Gregory. p12–13 – Vladimir Mucibabic, 1STudio.az. p14–15 –Viktor Hladchenko, UfaBizPhoto. p16 – Shutterstock.

Can you sort these words into two groups? One group has g as in **got**. One group has g as in **giant**.

Giant

Got

Magic

Huge

Gems

Get

Good

Magic is about using props to do a trick that makes it seem as if something magical has happened.

If you want to do magic, you can use cards, coins, flowers, gems, and a magic wand. Some people use hats and giant rabbits!

For some magic tricks, you must hide your hands and trick people so that they cannot see what you do with them.

A good trick is to hide a coin in your hand. If you adjust it a little bit, you can make it look like you got it out of someone's ear.

You can use cups to do magic. One trick is to make something go from one cup to a different cup.

You can amaze people with a deck of playing cards. You might tell someone to pick a random card and then tell them which card they picked.

You can use giant cards to do tricks. You need to be extra clever to do this. It is much harder to do things with these cards without people seeing.

Trained animals are sometimes used in magic tricks. Can you get a huge rabbit out of a hat? Or a bird from your sleeve?

For this magic trick, you need magic rings. The magic rings can be forced together until they are linked.

You can get someone to look at the rings to see if there are gaps in the rings. Hit them together so people can see there are no gaps.

In this trick, it seems as if something is floating. Some people can even make it seem as if they are floating!

When you do magic, you can hide how you do each trick. This makes the magic seem real to people who do not do magic.

Say the name of each object below. Is the "g" in each a /g/ sound or a /j/ sound?

ghost

grapes

angel

gems